CLIFF CLARIFIES THE BUSINESS BASICS

By

CLIFF HARDCASTLE, OBE FIET

To Jill my Wife of 53 years who put up with all the dangers without complaint.

CONTENTS

ACKNOWLEDGMENTS

To all my Bosses and colleagues that I worked with
and trained me for free.

INTRODUCTION

These suggestions and anecdotes derive from 62 years in business, working for 7 companies and creating 27 of my own from start-up to Stock Exchange flotation.

1. DECIDE WHAT REASONS COULD MAKE YOU WISH TO START YOUR OWN ENTERPRISE

Become rich? Be in charge? Be secure? Curiosity? Be famous? Be independent?

It is quite important to think about these and any other reasons you may have to start your own company. Also decide whether you are going to do it alone or with other people, either as partners or shareholders.

For my part it was a combination of being independent and in charge.

I was by many standards quite late in starting a company at 38 years old. I was finally pushed into it by working for an extremely strange and aggressive boss. I had known him for many years from when he had called on me as a salesman for a components company. At the time I was head of R&D at a

Westinghouse subsidiary. He suggested that engineers always get a bad break from companies and that I should consider my role in sales where the money and prestige would be much higher. Furthermore he made a very perceptive comment, saying that I had a specific talent for instilling trust in people. He said (and this was in the early 1960s) that people would trust me for half a million pounds. This turned out to be true and I had to rely on other people's trust many times to succeed and remain in business.

I joined his company at his invitation in 1971 to head up one of its sales departments. At that time I respected and admired him and his achievements. The company I came to him from had head-hunted me from Hewlett Packard to be a marketing manager and create more growth. If successful I would be promoted to a directorship and given a 10% shareholding. The growth was achieved but the Board then reneged on their promises with the excuse that as the company was now highly successful, the shares had become too valuable to give me the promised number.

I was thus looking for a change and an offer came at exactly the right moment, and seemed to be right for me. I didn't realise what a difficult boss he had turned into. He was to say the least a highly aggressive, controlling individual. He had an idea that working for a successful company meant accepting that its needs took precedence over private needs. Even up to the idea that if moved to the USA from the UK, you would have a new family provided in the USA to replace your English one! He would ring late on a Saturday or even early on a Sunday to discuss a new idea. He expected you to drop everything and start work. The final straw was during a business trip abroad, where he made the statement that nothing was impossible if enough effort was applied. I jokingly suggested that he tried pushing toothpaste back into the tube. He took violent exception to this and launched into a tirade that went on into the early hours. I met him for breakfast the following morning and he apologised, saying that if he ever did the same thing again I should remind him about this episode. It did reoccur and I reminded him of the episode, which launched him to even higher levels of aggression.

There was nothing to do but leave. Without realising it I had entered a deep depression. I thought I was coping very well and it took my courageous wife to get me to understand what a pit I was in mentally and physically. I was just sitting and watching television without talking. As she put it, I was no longer the man she had married. Over several discussions I came to the conclusion that I had to start my own company to get any peace of mind. We discussed the risks and to her great credit my wife supported the move even if it could cause us to move back to a smaller terraced house.

The move worked out and over a period of some months my mood and energy levels returned to normal. I will deal with the actual start and methodology later.

All that follows had to be learnt as I progressed.

2. UNDERSTAND THE MAIN BUSINESS IMPERATIVES

a) Do you have a product that people want to buy?

Without doubt this is the single most important influence on the successful creation of a new company. In fact there are several layers to this evaluation. For example, there are things that people HAVE to buy, e.g. Road Tax/TV Licence. There are other things that people NEED to buy e.g. food/water. And finally, there are products that people LIKE or WANT to buy, such as jewellery. If you have a product that people HAVE to buy, lucky you, the world is your oyster. Most of us have products that people want or like to buy. In the consumer field, it covers clothes, cameras, cars, etc. In the industrial/commercial field the product will need to have some unique or special capability that separates it from others. It may only be a perceived or an imagined difference but for future success it is vital that it has a clearly established benefit to the customer. This is dealt with later in a series of articles.

I have a multitude of examples of both successful and unsuccessful products, all of which at the time excited me and my colleagues.

Within the consumer field there was one totally outstanding example which illustrates what a complex and torturous process this can be. I had established my first company (Perdix Components Ltd) as an industrial component sales company specialising in new and advanced technologies, which required much engineering knowledge to sell. It was progressing, but slowly. One of my non-exec partners was a Hi-Fi enthusiast and he had discovered a new small bookshelf-mounting loudspeaker. It had exceptional merit but it was manufactured in Hungary, which at the time was still ruled by the USSR.

It so happened that my first job in industry after leaving the RAF was for Philips, designing Hi-Fi amplifiers and similar products. I had spent many years on this and gained a large amount of knowledge and listening skills. Although it had been some years since this work I had retained these capabilities. When I listened to this little speaker it had outstanding capability. I had never sold into the consumer market but didn't see that as a difficulty.

First I had to get the franchise to sell the product in England. I approached the Hungarian Embassy and made an appointment to see the appropriate official, a Mrs Kovesdy, wife of one of the commercial secretaries. I met her at the Embassy and she had the most stunning eyes I had ever seen, and I knew immediately that I would like to sell these speakers in large volumes, but actually at that stage only wanted a pair of samples for my colleague. My inexperience soon surfaced as Mrs Kovesdy asked how many I could buy. I had no idea! So I said eight pairs, depending on price. She then said the price was £6 a pair. The existing competitors sold for over £100 a pair so I got interested. She also said that eight pairs was not enough. At that price it wasn't a big issue but I knew that they made other larger sizes and rapidly added that I meant eight pairs of each type. At this she was happy and confirmed we could have the sole franchise depending on our performance over the following year.

After delivery of the eight sets of samples I listened to them and came to the conclusion that the small speakers, 'Minimax11', were exceptional, but the others were just about okay. We then placed a stocking order valued about £8,000 (to us a great deal of money at the time). I offered our industrial salesmen a generous bonus to sell these to Hi-Fi shops in their lunch time. WE SOLD NOTHING. We had no publicity and were unknown so the shops wouldn't take a risk based on their own judgement. I decided to take a space at the Hi-Fi exhibition in Harrogate. I had past experience of such events when working as a design engineer with Phillips.

In the meantime the Board had decided to get out of the speaker business and required me to sell the stock at any price I could get to recover some money.

During the exhibition the editor of a major Hi-Fi magazine talked to me and said that they had used the Minimax11 in a review, and that we would be pleased with the outcome. It was now August and the review was due out in October. I decided to ignore the Board's instruction and wait for the revue to be published. A good (fantastic) decision. The review, when published, showed that they had compared our speaker with 9 others, all more expensive and some multiple times our price. The review stated that the Minimax11 outperformed all the others by a big margin.

The following day orders flooded in. At that time our offices were in an end terrace house with a small extension and no warehouse. As a result the speakers were stored in the main passageway, the toilets, and the bathroom. Since the electricity meter was in the passageway it hadn't been read for many months. Finally we could get to the meter and celebrated by sharing in a bottle of cheap champagne.

We placed increasing orders and in my innocence I reprinted the review as an advert in other magazines. It did not carry a statement that it was an advert (now obligatory) and readers thought it was a new review. This accelerated orders even more. We found that being out of stock became an advantage. Our prospective customers visited shop after shop asking for the Minimax11. As a result the shops saw a bigger demand than was actual and placed even more advanced orders which caused them to preferentially sell against their outstanding orders.

THEN DISASTER. The government announced that VAT would be increased to 25%. Distraught shops rang us up to buy more stock but we had none. We offered that if we invoiced them immediately and they paid in cash immediately we could do this at the lower VAT, and we would then deliver the speakers when the next stock came in. The following Monday there was over £40,000 in cash in the mail lying on the front mat and it continued to pour in until the deadline. This amount of cash in 1974 was major and transformed our whole financial position.

We had created a product that PEOPLE WANTED TO BUY. And we knew how it worked.

We formed a new company to deal in Hi-Fi products and it made a lot of money. Ultimately we were selling other items, but none matched the Minimax11 performance and ultimately even its sales declined due to activities of the major retailers. We had a chain of about 150 independent dealers who did not discount. The major chains saw the popularity of the Minimax11 and wanted to sell them at a large discount. To me this was stupid. We had the fastest selling product that was already at a low price. Why discount it? So we did not sell through them. We had underestimated their knowledge and skills. Despite not having our speakers they still advertised them at a discount. When customers tried to buy them they switch sold them to another brand. Our independents saw the adverts and believed we had reneged on our promises and stopped ordering them. As a result sales dropped and we ultimately sold the business to Richer Sounds and concentrated on the industrial market, which was my main interest.

b) Do you know why they want to buy it?

We knew why people wanted to buy the Minimax11. It was because it had been designated a best buy by an authoritative magazine, and we got lucky with timing. However, it was not always the case that we knew why certain products sold well above normal expectations.

One early product where this was true was a range of advanced power supplies made by a firm in Colorado called Tecnetics, which included a range of high voltage units. I had decided that we should specialise in high voltage products as they were technically difficult and specialised, with high prices. I got the exclusive franchise for the Tecnetics range and started to advertise them. Orders came in immediately, but not for the high voltage range. At first I didn't pay any real attention but eventually the business became significant and from several different customers.

I decided to find out the reason behind these unexpected orders and made special visits to the bigger customers. One of these was Elliot Brothers at Rochester Airport. I pretended that my visit was a routine one but eventually got round to asking what they felt were the main features that our products brought them. To my astonishment what they were buying were special products aimed at the airborne market. The Tecnetic range was by far the smallest and lightest on the market. Elliot Brothers had several military contracts where they were the solution to major space and weight problems.

Once again I had got lucky. I wasn't alone however, because the president of Tecnetics (Myron C. Pogue – a truly memorable name) decided to come over from Colorado to find out how we were selling so many of these power supplies. He couldn't understand it so he came to England to find out how we were succeeding so well, and a long-term business was founded.

A different success came from a mistake made by one of our LCD suppliers, Sanyo. We had asked for a large LCD display to be made at half the size. We meant the same characteristics in a smaller space. That was misunderstood to mean cutting the display in half, and so reducing its resolution in half. We were disappointed but decided to see if anyone needed it, and placed adverts.

Once again it sold surprisingly well. We found they had a special application in medical heart care instruments. Doctors used large heartbeat monitors to look at the shape and repetition of a patient's heartbeat. They wanted to see the same shape and size on portable devices but regular LCD screens distorted them, so the doctors could not be certain of what they were seeing. With our new accidentally produced LCD the heartbeat shape was identical to the main machine. No competitor had anything the same and nobody understood how to do it. The whole market was ours.

These two examples show how sometimes a product sells for unknown reasons. However it is vital that if this happens you should find out the facts and thus promote and sell the product more fully.

Against these good luck products there were innumerable others that didn't sell, despite us believing that we had created a winner. I will write about those later and how to deal with arising problems. The main point to remember is that if you are wrong, get out of the situation as quickly and cheaply as possible. It can be a big mistake to soldier on spending money with a failing product. My sale of the Minimax11 to Richer Sounds is an illustration. He could make a success of it because he had his own shops. We didn't and couldn't sell as a result.

c) Do you know how to sell it?

SELLING is probably the most underrated and most ignored process in the UK. I say UK because there are other countries, notably the USA and Japan, where it is highly regarded and done well.

As illustrated in the preceding section we often did not know how to sell a product and even sometimes why it sold itself. The first job I had which concentrated on selling was with Hewlett Packard Scientific Instruments. This was before they became hugely involved with computers, and this original section has changed its name a couple of times since I left it. At that time they were the pre-eminent scientific/electronic instrument manufacturers in the world. As salesmen we had to be qualified engineers and fully understand the technology of all the individual instruments. This was because all our customers were engineers themselves and they expected us to be able to use and demonstrate any instrument that they were interested in.

Despite this technical expertise we were also sent on sophisticated sales training exercises so that we could vary our approach to each individual customer to match his personality as well as his technical needs. Some people buy a product to look good or seem important. Engineers in general buy for proven and safe performance. It can be fatal to tell and engineer that he will be the first to use a new technique, whereas an ambitious fast-rising manager may well grab at such an opportunity.

Later, working for other companies including my own (Densitron), I continued to go to training courses, some of which were residential and of two weeks' duration. I regularly forget what I have learnt, but when I am up against a real sales problem I find I can go back to these fundamentals and often uncover a solution which had previously eluded me.

Hewlett Packard also had strong and detailed sales management procedures. Each individual salesman had a defined territory (area) for which he had personal responsibility. The country was not only divided into sales areas but these were also collected into several regions containing roughly six sales areas, and there was a regional sales manager in charge of each region. His role was to supervise, encourage and train the salesmen. Each salesman worked from home and was heavily discouraged from going into the office, which in any case for me was a long journey across London.

Each salesman had to average five calls a day with a demonstration of an instrument counting as three calls. Each visit was reported on a daily report which noted the visits, the name of the contacts, the instruments discussed/demonstrated.

Alongside this we had to forecast the sales value arising from each call. This was aggregated by the regional manager and used to check whether you were likely to reach your sales targets. We also maintained a card index system, which had a card for each contact, recording all discussions with him so that we could maintain coherence and continuity during our visits over the course of a year or longer.

We also used a duplicate book for requesting action from the office staff. These duplicates had to be posted in daily and were coloured pink so that they stood out on desks, needing immediate action. This of course was in the days before mobile phones and tablet computers. However the same disciplines are relevant today, only the methodology needs change, especially communication.

All this has been about process and we now need to look at *sales messages* and *product branding*. A very large majority of products or services can be described using three words (characteristics), these are FEATURES, ADVANTAGES and BENEFITS. There is a tendency for most people to concentrate on the FEATURES of a product. For example with cars: fuel economy, engine size, colour, top speed etc. The advantages may be a lower cost of travel, good acceleration, easily seen on a motorway, or getting somewhere faster.

The BENEFITS would be: more money to spend on other things, overtaking more safely, less wear on the engine, being safer in poor light on the motorway, and more time to spend at the location.

As another example, take soap. The main FEATURE is that it lowers the surface tension of water (not an interesting sales message). The ADVANTAGE is that dirt leaves a surface more easily (also not a sales message). The BENEFITS are that you feel clean and don't smell, and these are really why most people buy scented toilet soap.

Therefore, for a successful sales campaign, you must clearly understand the BENEFITS that your product or service offers to potential customers. These MUST in some way be incorporated in your brand or sales message.

At Densitron I created a sales message that was easily understood and remembered. This was **N**ovel **E**ngineering **W**orldwide **S**ales – 'NEWS'. Our stated benefits were that we offered unique and better solutions and made them available on a worldwide basis. The worldwide part was especially interesting to large multinational companies.

We have now seen that sales organisation is an essential part of selling, as is knowing the products' benefits.

The benefits these two things bring are efficiency and focus.

Another major part of selling is the route you intend or need to get to your customers. If you have consumer products, are you going to sell directly, say by the internet or mail order catalogues? Are you going to sell through wholesalers to retailers or retailers directly? Will you need to have a sales force or regional stocking distributors?

In modern commerce the use of internet based sales techniques has revolutionised sales procedures. This a new; fast changing and growing area of activity. It is beyond the scope of this book to deal with properly. A separate paper will be issued shortly.

You should consider *franchising* as a business. You can take a franchise from an existing supplier or choose maybe to offer franchises for your product to other people. Franchising is a simple idea but is complex in its operation. There is a section later in this book dealing with this subject.

Each of these routes will require a different pricing structure and will be covered in the section dealing with finance. It is vital to know what margins these third party specialists need. It is rarely small.

If you are working in the industrial arena, sales tend to be organised on a more business to business route, although there are stockists and distributors. Once again, pricing will have to take account of working through third parties.

d) Can you (or should you) make or source it?

Your product may be your own design, in which case you can consider making it yourself and the implications of this are discussed later in pricing and profit discussions. Alternatively you can have it made for you by a specialist manufacturer. This may or may not be a higher cost route.

Making your products overseas in a low cost area may on the surface provide a large cost saving. However, you will need to place large orders and pay by some secured method, such as a Letter of Credit. There will also be transport costs and handling fees by importing agents. Accounting for these extra costs, may increase the final price and they will also have an effect on your cash flow.

For example we (Densitron) had at one time two

highly successful product areas. These were LCD displays and electromechanical solenoids. These were manufactured in Japan. The LCDs were lightweight and had a high price. In consequence, we could transport them by air, resulting in little added relative cost. Consequently the prices and delivery cycle were low and short. As a result they sold equally well in Europe and America.

The solenoids by comparison, were heavy and carried a relatively low price. In order to make a good profit they were transported by sea. Travelling from Tokyo to Los Angeles took only a few days and thus had little impact on our delivery cycle. Coming to Europe however, was a different matter as the journey time rose to between six and eight weeks. Our customers required regular monthly deliveries, which meant that at one time we would be waiting on average two months for payment of goods delivered, plus one month's delivery in our warehouse. There would be two months' worth on ships at sea and one months' production underway in the factory. A total of six months' finance exposure and cash flow stress. Until we reduced these problems our sales of solenoids in Europe remained low. There are many variants of this conundrum but the overriding problem will usually be that of cash flow rather than profit.

The choices next available are to have it made locally, or alternatively by making it yourself in your own facilities. Having others make it locally is the easiest but you have to have a purchasing system that can manage the whole ordering and delivery cycle. Having it made by others locally can in some circumstances create a new competitor. It is vital that you have control of your Intellectual Property rights, an issue that I discuss in section 'h'.

e) How many do you need to sell to make a profit? How to calculate price?

This is without doubt the most complex and variable decision making process. An old saying, which is the underlying truth, is that COST IS A FACT, PRICE IS AN OPINION.

Costings are relatively straightforward tasks. If you buy in a product or have one made to your design, the cost will be decided by the price asked by the supplier. Obviously the better negotiator you are the better price you will be able to get. Buying in larger amounts at a time should lead to a lower purchasing cost. Also, the price you pay will depend on market forces and any special financial arrangements you offer can reduce the price.

Examples being '*Cash with Order*', a '*Letter of Credit*', or '*Promissory Note*'. On the other hand there may be upward pressure caused by the cost of raw materials, transport costs, inflation and exchange rates. So the cost of buying in a product is very clear, but there are many factors that can change with time. I deal with most of these issues in the financial section of this document, where there is space to deal with what is a very complex subject.

In larger organisations there are specialist jobs for buying, and they are senior posts.

If you 'buy in' make certain you understand the contractual terms you are agreeing to which may allow variances with time or quality. If you decide to make the product yourself, you will have to calculate the cost of doing so in a totally disciplined way to include any financing or property costs and any wages, etc., for the workers involved. These calculations are dealt with fully in our section dealing with *Finance and Accounting*. Having determined costs, you can start on the more dynamic and difficult process of deciding your sales price.

The underlying calculation for determining your sales price is what is called the GROSS MARGIN. Put simply, **the gross margin is the sales price less the cost of acquiring the basic product**. If, for example, you buy in a product for an in-store cost of £10 and sell it for £15, the gross margin is £5. This represents a 50% mark up on the sales price, or alternatively a 33.3% margin on the sales price.

Why is this so important? It is because you must cover all your overhead costs from this gross margin. This is the extra money that you create to enable you to earn a salary, pay employees, advertise, pay rent, pay accountants and lawyers, pay taxes etc. By knowing your gross margin you can carry out financial planning. An example of typical overhead structure is given later in the section on FINANCIAL RECORDING AND MEASUREMENTS.

An example of a Price Calculation for a bought-in item.

The ex-factory price is £10 from your supplier, add transport + storage + financing, making the cost price increase to £13, sometimes this is called the prime cost.

To this you have to add your own expected annual costs or OVERHEADS. These include the salaries of you and your staff – £50k. To this add premises + finance & banking + advertising + phones and computers + cleaning, professional services, adding up extra costs to approximately £42,000 per year.

Thus total costs will be £50k + £42k, or £92k. Obviously these costs will be spread out over the whole year and you should prepare a cash flow statement that details this on a monthly basis.

CALCULATIONS

First Example: Buy or make product for £13 and sell it for £26, giving a gross margin of 50% or £13.

In order to cover 1 year costs (break even without paying any salaries) you will need to sell £42000 ÷ 13 = 3230 units. Or 269 per month, or 68 per week.

To buy 3230 units at £13 will cost £42k. Thus, your total annual expenditure on products and overhead will be £84,000

Second Example: Buy for £13, sell for £20, a

gross margin of 30% or £7.

You will have to sell 6000 units per year at a cost of £78,000, giving an annual expenditure of £120,000.

Third Example: Buy for £13 and sell for £17 at a gross margin of 24%, you have to sell 10,500 units and total costs will be £178,000.

This short example gives a clear indication of the impact of varying gross margins and overheads on the financing needed. You must remember that these calculations provide you with a minimum annual income and no retained profit for expansion. This model will not attract outside investors and bank loans will need personal guarantees.

There is one story from my personal experience that illustrates the strategic nature of pricing (price is an opinion), I learnt it at Hewlett Packard (the source of much of my useful knowledge). I had been appointed as specialist sales manager for a totally new product conceived, designed and built at our factory in South Queensferry, Scotland. As sales manager I was asked to attend the pricing meeting at the factory. This was a first as in my previous experience sales people were told what price to sell a product at.

The meeting started with a rigorous listing of all the costs, which in itself was extremely informative as I had not had a chance previously to understand the nature of the true cost of building a new product. This included the R&D expenditure, the cost of the invested capital, the basic cost of assembly, and the cost of all the labour associated with putting it into stores. HP at that time made in batches that reflected the actual and expected sales volume. Then with all these costs established, the in-store cost was a known amount.

The finance managers then illustrated what the required return on invested capital was and how this would be met at varying sales volumes depending on pricing. After this, a minimum price for a proper return was established. In this case it came to £1900 per unit. I relaxed and was very happy that at last I understood pricing.

I forgot this was the mighty Hewlett Packard; pre-eminent scientific instrument maker in the world. The MD turned to me and in a fairly quiet voice asked me what I thought would be the maximum price that I could sell it at. In my innocence I replied that in my opinion its absolute unacceptable maximum would be £5000. I then said that pricing it at £4900 would avoid seeming expensive and would sell well. "Right," replied the MD, "that is the price at which we will sell it. You, Cliff, have said that you can sell it at this price. Go and do it."

The cost was defined and the price was my opinion. Luckily it did sell well at that price. I gained a good reputation from this and impressed both the MD and Finance Director in this process, and ultimately somewhat later they became initial investors in Densitron.

f) Can you finance it? Will you need investment capital and/or loan capital?

There is little doubt that this subject dominates all new or fast changing companies and is a major cause of worry to managers and directors. In the course of building Densitron I had to use virtually every form of financing that exists.

These were 'Personal Savings', investment in shares made by outside personal contacts, borrowing from family members, bank overdrafts, bank loans secured against company assets, bank loans secured against the value of my house, hire purchase, factoring, Letters of Credit from us to suppliers and to us from customers, Promissory Notes, personal guarantees, credit terms agreed with suppliers, Cash with Order, late payment of invoices, floating on the UK Stock Exchange, issuing rights issues to existing shareholders, and borrowing from shareholders.

Despite this long list of financial sources there are at its basics only two sorts of money that exist in either personal or company finances. These are fixed capital investment (money that is yours) and loans (money lent to you for a period but that has to be repaid).

It is vital to understand the role of fixed capital invested in a company either by the owners alone or by other outside investors. The amount of capital invested in a company is in a major way a statement of your confidence. You can start a Limited Liability Company with only £1 share capital but this shows to the outside world how little confidence you have in the company. A serious company will seek to have good enough share capital to underpin a company's finance in a difficult time. For a growing company creating good profits, it is good practice to retain some of each year's profits which can be added to the issued share capital.

Banks and other financial companies will lend money against the issued share capital and suppliers will offer better credit terms to a soundly financed company. One interesting measurement of a company is the return (profit) made on the investor's capital. If it is less than you can get from putting your money in the bank, then you are not performing well.

MONEY

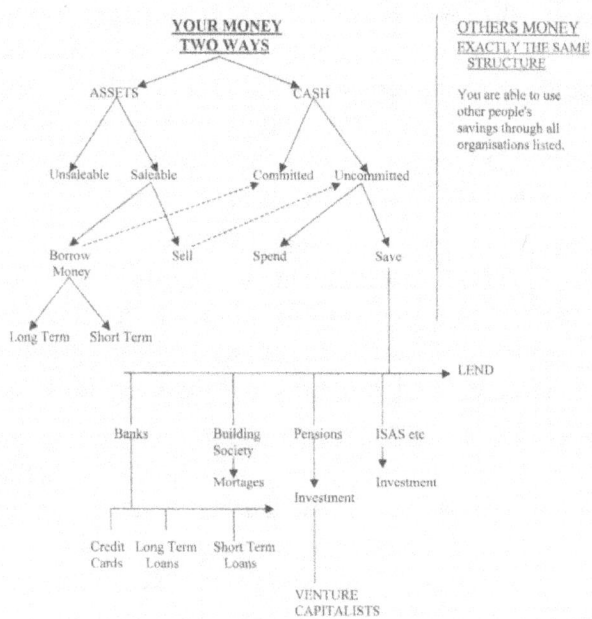

TWO WAYS TO LOOK AT MONEY

(Taken from my article 'From the Boardroom'.
July 2004)

A couple of weeks ago I had the pleasure of being invited to address a joint Anglo-French seminar on financing and growing biotech companies, which was being held in Lille. It was a very interesting event held in the revitalised town of Lille – lots of EU money having been spent! It was an extremely encouraging example of how Anglo-French cooperation works extremely well at grass roots. Maybe it is only at the national political level that there is any difficulty.

The easy camaraderie and helpful attitude between the two nations was quite exemplary and I must commend the French, in particular, for having carried out the whole two days in English. Imagine the problem if it had been held in French!

However, as the two days wore on, a great deal of the discussion was about Venture Capital funding and it became obvious to me that in general people didn't understand money and I tried to come up with a simple explanation of what money is about and why Venture Capitalists are such tricky people. This article gives you my deliberations. The small diagram further in the article enables you to see the whole picture in an easy way.

What I came to realise was that there are always two ways to look at money and once you realise that the step process to arrive at the different stages of money is relatively simple.

The first decision is that *there are two sorts of money in the world*, and only two. There is *the money you have* and *the money everybody else has*. Let us examine the money you have because it will provide an insight into the money that other people have. The money you have breaks down again into two parts. One is **cash** and the other **assets**. So let's start with **CASH**. There are two forms of cash. One is cash that you owe or have committed in some way and the other is cash that you are free to spend. And that is the really interesting bit and will come back to it in a moment.

Returning to the **assets** side of life, there are two sorts of assets and only two. Those that you can sell and those that you can't. There is little you can do with those assets you can't sell. But the assets you can sell break into two opportunities. You can either sell them, in which case the proceeds go up into free cash or you can take a loan against them, in which case it goes to committed cash. It's as simple as that. There are no other forms of money other than the short list above. You can get into some sophistication, but at the end of the day that is it, that is the total description of money belonging to you.

The really interesting thing is, that list of items is the same for other people's money. They have exactly the same ownership tree in terms of cash and it is no more complicated than that. The only thing is that on the other side of the coin, there will be people who are richer than you, and people who are poorer than you. What you are basically interested in, of course, are the people who are richer than you and finding some way to get access to their money.

Let us, therefore, return to the free cash in your hands and what you do with it. Basically it goes into two ways again. You can either spend it on things you want or you can save it in some form. And it is the savings I want to talk about at this point.

If you decide to save or invest your money, you will put it in the hands of somebody else. That will be a bank, your pension fund, building society, investment broker or something of that nature. It may be of course that if you are particularly generous, or an exciting person to know, you will be prepared to invest your money directly in other people's enterprises. If you are a rich person and do this you are known as a 'business angel' and can be a joy to know. On the other hand you might be less rich but a member of the family or friend, in which you can often be persuaded to put up capital investment funds into the companies.

However, the bulk of all this money goes into banks, building societies, pension funds or investment trusts. They in turn have to make a return on the money that has been basically lent to them in the form of surplus cash of other people. The demands on them are to provide an ongoing return for the people who have lent them their money and they also have to earn enough money for themselves to make their living worthwhile. That is why the city people like to operate with large sums of money because it makes them able to earn larger sums for themselves, whilst still showing some form of return to the original investor.

Venture Capitalists come after this. They will dream up a scheme that will make money in a relatively short time but hopefully in big bucket loads. They will take their proposition to pension funds, banks and all the other structures that exist in the city and persuade them to invest in the Venture Capital fund, which usually has a five-year life. It has to start its business, invest its money, earn their keep and return the money with profits within a five-year scale. Naturally it takes time to investigate various propositions and it can be that when you get to meet a Venture Capital fund they are already three years into their five-year fund and are looking to make a return in just the two years that are left. If you don't have a proposition that meets these requirements, you have no chance. There are Venture Capitalists who indulge in what is called 'fund of funds', that is, they will borrow from other Venture Capital funds to obtain money for even more exotic ventures because now they will have to produce a return for the original investor, the intermediary holder, the previous Venture Capital fund and their own Venture Capital fund. So these people will demand extremely high returns and will only finance such things as massive management buy-outs or buy-ins.

In these circumstances you can see that to persuade people to give you money on a long-term basis will require a good business offer to them to make it worth their while to put risk capital in your hands, and it is not easy to get that. It is easier to obtain loans of one form or another because effectively all the money that these various institutions have is on a loan basis. The reason they will invest in public companies is because theoretically the shares are easily traded and therefore they can turn their shares into cash at any appropriate moment to return to the original investor if he requires it.

When the smaller companies amongst you to borrow money, you should understand that it is only loaned to you on behalf of other people. There are a wide variety of loan schemes available that you can use to help finance your business. Consider such mechanisms as hire purchases, leasing, Bills of Exchange, Letters of Credit, overdrafts, term loans, etc. and against the right security will provide you with a great deal of working capital. You can borrow the money usually against the company's assets, your own assets, or under certain circumstances with certain types of money it can be secured against the business transaction itself. For example, Letters of Credit can be raised in the right circumstances, back-to-back with guarantees from the customer or even the supplier. There is also factoring which is often an under-utilised facility offered by nearly all banks. This is where the factoring company will advance you money against the security of the invoices to creditworthy customers. There are a wide variety of schemes and you would have to investigate them fully to determine if they are suitable for you but they can be extremely valuable for companies that receive sporadic very large orders.

From all of this you can see that money itself is not that complicated. All there is, is **yours** and **theirs** assets or cash. Nothing else. The only difficulty you really have is to get your sweaty little palms on a big enough slug of it for as long as you want, and therein lies the art of investment and creating companies.

In my career building Densitron, availability of money was always a dominant issue. I have to say that at first I was not very knowledgeable about the use of money in a business. None of the companies that I had worked for had provided any training. Luckily I had an outstanding local accountant who took time to advise me and identify a local bookkeeper who was available for work. This being before the availability of small computers, she wrote by hand into five ledgers. These were (1) Purchase Day Book, (2) Purchasers Ledger, (3) Sales Day Book, (4) Sales Ledger, (5) General Ledger.

From these I was able to understand the dynamics of the flow of money through the company. It clearly identified how much money we were owed and how much we owed to others. It was only by collecting the money owed to us that we could pay our creditors on time and maintain certainty of supply and an outstanding reputation for on-time payment with our suppliers. I became very aggressive in getting paid, even by large companies such as Plessey and Philips. I was always very polite but very, very firm and it worked. Early on in my company's existence, I once sat in front of the finance director of a Plessey subsidiary who owed us several months' money. I explained to him that mine was a very small company funded by my savings and a mortgage on my house. If Plessey did not pay on time I would go broke and my family would become homeless. I asked him to look me in the eye and say he approved of that outcome. To his great credit he not only paid then and there but for years afterwards we got paid on time.

g) How can you raise finance?

Before you seek to obtain money you should spend time working out exactly what you want it for, how long you will need, and how much you need. This is usually an integral part of a business plan, which you should create in the first place. These days if you try to raise money from traditional routes such as Venture Capitalists or other individual investors they will expect a coherent business plan that shows clearly how their investment will earn a return each year and how they will be able to sell their investment after, say, three to six years at a significant capital profit. You need to understand what fixed capital investment you will require and how much variable working capital (trading money) you will use.

I didn't do any of this because I had no idea it might be needed. In my early years I tended (and sometimes still do) to just blunder onwards using what I think is common sense. As I succeeded very well it may be worth telling the story as it developed.

The real start came when in my early 30s I was interviewed for a post as area salesman at Hewlett Packard. This was when they made the best scientific instruments in the world and before they made computers. The final stage was being interviewed by the MD, Dennis Taylor. He invited me to tell him what job I would ultimately aim at in HP if selected. I replied that I would aim at his job and if I didn't succeed I would set up my own company. His immediate response was that IF I should ever set up my own company, he would like to be involved and told me to contact him at the right time.

Subsequently, he had a friend with a small electronics company, RBS Capacitors, making passive components. Dennis took me along to see his factory and check whether I could give any advice to help it grow. The owner, George Lee, had acquired the company by accident and wasn't a qualified engineer. Consequently I was able to make some useful comments. He again expressed interest in any new company I started.

Eventually I left HP (the best company I have ever worked for) through being head-hunted to become marketing director at KGM, a small specialist electronic displays manufacturer. Although again I left them as they reneged on the promises they had made me. I joined Guest International which was a big but productive mistake and led to my depression, which in turn pushed me into starting my own company.

Through these last two companies I had learnt how to import products from around the world and how to create a brand name. I decided to become a very technical and specialised importer of advanced electronic components. I decided on components rather than manufactured equipment because if you sold one component into a prototype, larger orders would follow as the product advanced into production without having to sell again each time a new batch was made. On the other hand selling, say, scientific instruments, it was necessary to keep finding new customers for individual items which would need repair and warranties.

That decided, I had only £3000 of savings and a large ambition, which I instinctively felt was not enough. I decided to go and talk to George Lee, who I was still in touch with. I intended to work from home but George offered to give me a part-time paid job on the basis that I sold his products more widely. I took the job because it would help eke out my savings and it was a real company rather than my intended one. Unbeknown to me George phoned Dennis Taylor that evening telling him about these events. Dennis immediately phoned me and suggested that he should come down to discuss my plans and bring with him John Penrose, the Finance Director of HP UK. He further asked me to do nothing until he and John had met with me.

I had no problems with this as I had actually not done anything except meet George Lee. Ultimately Dennis and John came to my home and made the proposition that they would invest in the new company. I was flattered and appreciative that two such eminent people wanted to back me. At that stage I had no company, no bank account, and exceptionally, no products to sell. I agreed and their involvement and connections ultimately paid off big time, although sometimes even they did not realise the effect they could have. This was especially the case with banking. We went to the Bank of Scotland who were HP's bank in Edinburgh. Later on when we needed some large sums of money, they backed us, fearing not to do so would cause them to lose the HP account. We made no such stipulations and indeed they never occurred to us.

Friends and Family

You will find that most advice about raising initial funds suggests that the first port of call should be friends and family. This was certainly the case for me although bank funding became our dominant source of funds. I was once supported by my father-in-law at a very critical stage in the early business. He gave me a personal loan that secured the supply of a crucial product from Japan that underpinned our business for some years afterwards. The product was an advanced digital display that I had introduced and imported whilst still working for another company two years earlier. The Japanese manufacturer offered to switch the exclusivity to us, provided we bought a large quantity by advanced payment in YEN for the whole consignment. There were enough units for nearly six months' supply and the bank would not lend money against them because of the uncertainty involved. My father-in-law's money covered it and it was a very generous act as there was no guarantee we could repay him. We did so, however, together with reasonable interest.

Financial Instruments

There was a side effect to this which came without me realising it happened or its eventual importance. Because we had bought such a large shipment by cash, in advance, my supplier and eventual partner Mr Degawa (Densitron) was able to get a Japanese Government (MITI) credit rating for us. This allowed him to export to us without pre-payment either in cash or by Letter of Credit, which virtually every other company importing from Japan had to provide. Because of our good credit rating Densitron sold to us using a Promissory Note. Basically this was a financial note we signed stating that we would pay on time. We were allowed 60 days to pay. The goods came by airfreight, taking about four days to get into our warehouse and we shipped them out the same day to the UK customer with 30 days credit. We made all customers stick rigidly to this and we pushed them hard to do so as most of the larger companies liked to take extended credit. As a result we had our cash in the bank when it came to pay the supplier. We were making a gross margin of 30% so were generating cash very strongly. We continued this process for many, many years and even at one stage added the use of factoring.

Factoring (or invoice discounting) is where you can sell your invoices to the factoring company for around 80% of the invoiced value and be paid within a few days. The remaining 20% was forwarded when the customer paid. The factoring company only covered sales to creditworthy customers and therefore we got free credit ratings for customers. We also paid extra to insure against bad debts if our customer defaulted for any reason not caused by us.

This process allowed us to buy from other Asian companies not using LOCs or Promissory Notes. Essentially we negotiated 30 days' credit from the supplier based upon our by now outstanding payment record. The factors paid to us 80% of the goods price which covered our basic purchase price. We were able to pay the supplier and have 20% held by the factors. We controlled our overheads to 20% and so almost all of our costs were still covered by the factoring process and we just waited for the final payment for our profit.

The total financing of a company is mostly much more complex than the system we used at this time, but without any doubt it all was solely down to our management of cash flow using these and other tools discussed elsewhere that we were able to grow to become a public company. Pretty well every accountant we employed tried to change these arrangements to more conventional financing. They especially disliked Factoring, which was regarded as the first stage of going bankrupt. This was largely based upon experiences in the clothing retail businesses, where fast moving trades could disrupt the cash flow disastrously. Its use in industry was unusual at that time and not liked by accountants except for the one who helped me float the company (Ian Sibson). Ian, although a qualified accountant, had worked elsewhere and had a finely tuned brain. He understood the whole thing and without him there would have been no DENSITRON plc. When we floated we had grown at 40% per annum for 14 years consecutively without having to yield any shares to others for financing. Try doing that without a thorough understanding of money (NOT ACCOUNTANCY). I deal with understanding accountants elsewhere.

These events cover the somewhat unconventional techniques that I used to build Densitron. I do not put them forward as a recommendation but more of an illustration of facts about raising money. This is that it is essential that the owners; non-financial senior managers and especially the technical side of the company such as engineers and salesmen understand '*money*' and have some knowledge of accountancy, which in essence is only an agreed set of rules to describe the financial situation of a company and is discussed later in this book.

I had earlier illustrated the idea that there are only two sorts of money and this holds true here. There is money you have, and all the rest belongs to someone else. No matter how rich you are the 'all the rest' will always be much, much bigger. If you want to borrow or use it there is a price and you should always, always check what that price will be.

Banks

Most people think of banks as the first port of call for money. The regular High Street banks use their depositors' money to make loans to companies. They do NOT invest. If you borrow from them it is not their money, it is their depositors', and they are not supposed to put it into unreasonable risk. They will need to understand what security exists for repayment if they lend you money. The riskier the situation, the more interest and charges will be imposed. If they see a real risk they will need you or the directors of a business to personally guarantee the repayment. They will tend to want you to provide a charge over any assets used as collateral, including your house if you have one. The reason credit cards and pay-day loans carry such high interest rates is because the security is low and the interest charged has to cover the inevitable failures to pay.

Banks and other institutions will lend money for the purchase of valuable assets such as cars and office equipment. They may also lend against your stock in the warehouse but you will pay higher interest levels. They will lend you for the purpose of property but you lose the property if you can't repay.

The only real long-term money is (for a Ltd company) shareholder funds. You lose some of the ownership value of the company when you issue shares to other people but you get the certainty of owning the money. Shareholders will expect two main things: a) an income in the way of dividends, and b) a capital gain if they sell the shares or the company is purchased by another company.

These comments are just as applicable to Venture Capitalists or Merchant Banks etc. They are investing to make money, helping you make money is secondary and really only a by-product of their requirements.

Much more recently have come the opportunities of *crowd funding* where small or start-up companies can raise very substantial sums through the internet and there are companies that specialise in carrying out the whole process. Many times the money will be raised against a special discount offer or service provided. Much more can be raised quickly by including riskier offers, provided they are interesting enough.

So there are many, many ways to raise money but once again always remember there are only two sorts of money, YOURS and THEIRS.

h) *Intellectual Property issues*

For a number of companies much of their value lies in what may be called *intellectual property*. These may be patents, copyrights, registered designs, logos and even names. This is a very complex area of both national and international law and I highly recommend you seek real professional advice if you have interests in protecting or using intellectual property at any time. In this short chapter I will cover some of the basic points but I am not competent to give professional advice.

Accountants tend to refer to intellectual property by calling it 'Intangible Assets'. In this way they can be given a value for the Balance Sheet but it is recognised that the value is based upon an opinion rather than demonstrated and recorded costs. However, despite being mostly based upon opinion, the value in intellectual property can make a difference in valuing a company which is huge compared to more regular items such as buildings and machinery.

PATENTS

This is the one intellectual property that most people are familiar with. Patenting an item requires some specific matters to be addressed. To patent an item you will have to use a patent agent/lawyer who will explain all the rules and the law as it is at the time you appoint them. Patent law does change and it varies internationally, and in these circumstances I will not try to guide you in these matters. The major point to patenting an item is that is must be totally new and show invention. This invention must be described in words (and drawings) as a claim. It is this or these claims that will be where most people start to check whether any infringement has happened.

Before your patent is granted, its details will be published for all to see. You have to describe what your invention is, and more importantly how it works. In this way all your competitors will be able to try and work out ways to avoid your patent.

You will have to pay for your patent claim to be examined, and if successful, to have it recorded. You may wish to patent in other countries. This will be very expensive.

Another issue is if you have large competitors they may choose to ignore your patent. If they do this you will have to sue them in court, which can become very expensive. If you can't pay for a court hearing, you lose and your patent is virtually useless. You can licence your patent to a richer organisation and let them fight the court battle. You will lose full control over your patent but you could well still make money through the licence. Be aware that a patent only has a limited lifeline and once that time has expired there is no longer any protection.

COPYRIGHT

Most people are aware of copyright especially with regard to books, documents, music etc. It is a very powerful protection especially because it is long-lasting and can continue for many years after the death of the person who created the documents. Copyright is automatically applied when the documents are created. If there is a dispute then the person who can show an original document properly dated with the earliest date is judged to own the copyright.

Copyright for a product will lie in the drawings and be held by the owner with the earliest dated drawings. That is why it is very important to date drawings or anything else that can carry an attested date. I met this problem when I discovered in Japan an innovative electromechanical 7-segment digital display. I negotiated the sales rights and proceeded to sell it and began to make good profits. I was unaware of the rules of copyright and knew no other display was constructed in the same way. I was contacted by an American company claiming copyright. I replied that our device was made by an entirely different technique. Unfortunately their copyright existed in the basic shapes of the display segments. They threatened to sue us globally unless we stopped selling it immediately. They were a much larger company than us at the time and we couldn't really afford a court battle in the USA. I asked to be sent the drawings so that I could verify their claim. They refused, saying if we wanted to see them it would be in court. End of story, and yet again an important lesson about the power of size in a legal dispute.

INDUSTRIAL DESIGN

This right protects the visual appearance of a

product that is not just utilitarian. It can comprise shape, colour, pattern and other similar features. Once again, expert advice is essential.

TRADEMARKS

A trademark distinguishes products or services from a particular source. It is usually a recognisable sign or expression drawn in a particular way.

TRADE DRESS and TRADE SECRETS

These are less widely used and I once again recommend going to an expert.

In summary, there are a range of tools available to enable you to protect your business, its name, its products and inventions, etc. The purpose of using these is to enable you to get the maximum benefit from running your business for the maximum duration of time. It is a complex area of law and my comments are only a guide as to the range of protection available, and you should seek expert advice at an early stage. Your protection will only be as good as your ability to finance a defence of your rights. Small companies will be at a severe disadvantage against much larger ones. In these circumstances an alliance with a friendly company by way of a licence may be a good way forward.

3. SEVEN GUIDELINES FOR A SUCCESSFUL BUSINESS

The idea of these objectives is to provide a simple framework on which daily decisions can be taken.

By writing down in order of importance the main reasons for the company to be in business, each employee is supplied with a simple check-list for decision making. If a difficult decision is to be made, then it should be checked against these objectives one by one. If it falls against any of the first two, it should be rejected. The best decision will meet all of these main objectives.

To a large extent the first objective of continuity covers all the following objectives. The company cannot be continuous if it falls on the other objectives.

1. Continuity

Everybody, customers, suppliers, employees, bankers, etc., needs the company to remain in continuous business. No decision should ever be taken which threatens the future effective operation of the company. For example, we should not spend too much money, cheat the tax requirements, make losses, employ criminals or lazy people. We should not take orders larger than we have money to finance. We must have enough new products and train ourselves for the future and be enthusiastic. **CONTINUITY is the number one priority**.

2. Profit

Profit is the reward we get for a well-run company. It rewards the employees with better pay and working conditions. It rewards the investors with dividends to encourage them to keep investing. It rewards the suppliers with bigger business, and it rewards customers with better products. However, more importantly, it provides the increased money for the company to grow into the future with the premises and people to run it properly.

3. Customers

Everybody understands that we need customers, but how do we get them and keep them? Firstly, we should look at the customer as somebody who needs to buy things to run their business. If we offer them products which are superior to the competition they will want to buy from us. So therefore, the main way to get customers is to offer them superlative and new products. To keep him we must back that product up with top grade service: salespeople who know the product and customer engineers who can answer the questions, a delivery service which gets the goods there in time, and a financial service which ensures the end result is timely and profitable. We must be seen by customers as an enthusiastic, caring, efficient supplier of modern competitive products.

4. Growth

For many reasons companies need to grow, but it is often difficult to decide by how much and then to actually achieve that growth. The most important reason to grow is that it is safer than not growing.

It is regarded that growth of Balance Sheet assets is the fundamental underpinning of all other forms of growth. Whilst obviously sales revenues and reported profits are important, it is the net asset situation on the Balance Sheet which is the specific determinate of growth. The security of the Balance Sheet should not be jeopardised in order to manipulate reported profits. By growing we can increase salaries, recruit new people with new ideas, encourage investors to continuously invest, and help our customers grow. We should aim to grow at being better than the rest of our industry, then we can be safe against decline or failure.

5. Our People

Basically, a company is only a theoretical concept. In reality it is a group of people working together for mutual benefit. Our policy is to encourage the most talented people to join the company at all levels. We then wish to tell them clearly what the company is trying to achieve and let them work within these guidelines to fulfil their own ambitions.

The Board of Directors have issued this set of objectives and then also a range of strategies and policies to help people meet the objectives. Each year each company or division writes down a forecast of achievable performance for the following year, and after agreement with the Board they set out to achieve this. In this way the people of the company help the company grow and secure for themselves a growing and satisfying career.

In the circumstances of the modern global economies, it is important that everybody accepts the need for continuous training to update and improve the skills within every individual. Such training is a joint responsibility and whilst the company should expect to lead in the matter, it is also required that every individual ensures that their training fits them for their role within the company.

6. Management

The management of a company is the method by which it organises its people to carry out its objectives. It is obviously necessary that everyone in the company goes in the same direction so that maximum results may be achieved. The directors of the company decide what the company is trying to achieve and then appoint various managers to carry out the agreed policies.

In my work I have given as much responsibility to each individual as possible by a system of setting objectives to achieve at all levels

(Management by Objectives)

It is not expected that every action is controlled by a central, powerful group issuing orders. My method is to encourage everyone to understand the overall company objectives as set out in this document and then arrange their own actions to follow the same path.

7. Citizenship

OBJECTIVE:

To honour our obligations to society by being an economic, intellectual and social asset to each nation and each community in which we operate. All of us should strive to improve the environment in which we live. As my corporation operates in many different communities throughout the world, we must make sure that each of those communities is better for our presence. This means identifying our interests with those of the community; it means understanding the uniqueness and qualities of other societies, and ensuring that through our contacts with them we improve mutual understanding. The wider our trade and the more independence and understanding we achieve, the more likely we are to achieve our own ambitions.

Wherever possible we should seek to make a contribution to whatever society we find ourselves working or living in. If we respect other people and their societies they will be more likely to respect ours. In turn our own self-respect will grow.

SPECIAL NOTES AND EXAMPLES

a) Do not risk going out of business. What are the common ways to go out of business?

Very special attention should be paid to the fact that you can be a highly profitable and growing company and still go out of business. HOW? Basically it comes down to not having enough free cash to pay your outstanding creditors. As an example, because you are growing fast and Christmas is coming you buy a larger volume of stock so that you will not miss the opportunity for extra sales. In the event if you do not sell as much as you expected, you are left with a large residue of stock to pay for. Because you didn't make the sales, you do not have the resulting anticipated profits as cash. You still have the stock at its purchase price so your Balance Sheet is showing you as solvent. Your suppliers choose not to wait and take you to court who order you to pay, and as you can't you are forced into insolvency. This scenario is much more common in one form or another than many people realise. I refer you back to the section of this book that illustrates the two forms that money can adopt.

The other major route to insolvency is bad debts, where companies owe you money and either won't pay you or can't do so. You should check the financial status of all potentially significant customers before selling to them. This is simple and cheap in the UK because of the information from Companies House on Limited companies. This cannot be so easily done for individuals or sole traders and you will have to follow other routes to avoid bad debts. You can buy insurance but it is not cheap. You can ask for payment in advance with a possible discount. I have already discussed Factoring or invoice discounting where the supplier of the service will stipulate credit ratings; one technique I used for smaller companies who lacked enough cash to guarantee payment but nonetheless had a profitable and growing business. I would persuade them not to place a large order with a single delivery, but instead place the order with weekly deliveries and payment on a weekly basis. One company that I helped in this way became very large and was targeted by our competitors offering lower prices. They did not change from us. We did not exploit the situation by keeping much higher prices and enjoyed many years of profitable business.

I suggest that a regular and comprehensive evaluation of your risks as a business is vital to your long-term survival. The trouble with risks is that they change all the time. What is considered important or even vital may change overnight (e.g. a new competitor) so constant vigilance and evaluation are essential to stay in business in the long term.

For an example I will use a subsidiary we had created and grown which was Densitron Microwave Ltd. It made parts for a range of microwave applications, but the biggest by far was to the then emerging mobile phone market. We had designed some very high technology metal parts that were used in the base stations of mobile phone networks. At that time the main market was in Scandinavia with companies such as Nokia and Ericsson. We had created not only the latest technology but had also by coincidence become the most competitive in price. Our main competition was other UK companies and we were able to take the lion's share of the business very profitably.

However, as is now clear this market was going to explode and attract the attention of larger international companies. Few of us smaller companies really saw the future, but we were clear that we lacked the financial muscle to keep investing in new designs and manufacturing capability. Our directors did have concerns about this, and with our Asian connections, realised that that big companies were getting involved. It was unlikely we could maintain our technical and price advantages or even the capital resources to invest. We came to the conclusion that although it was a very profitable part of our business we had to exit this market. Our timing was excellent because a new-ish large American company wanted to enter the European markets in the very immediate future. We negotiated a sale of our subsidiary which we had started in 1973 with £30k and sold at a price of around £8 million. This extra income helped us expand and invest in our displays business. If we had held on to that business we may have supervised a dramatic decline in our profitability and not found a buyer. Sometimes directors hang on to a business for too long when it becomes uncompetitive. On a national scale you can consider coal mining, ship building, steel manufacturing and car manufacturing.

b) Make a real profit, not a fabricated one

An understanding of the accounting profession will help illuminate this statement. As written earlier in this booklet the accounting profession has grown so strong because its activities are central and vital in describing the financial state of a company. These matters are dealt with much more fully later under the heading *FINANCIAL RECORDING AND MEASUREMENTS*.

I will not dwell on the full issues to consider but just advise you to understand how accountancy works and how profit is not always a clear issue. As a simple example, you could make good and substantial gain if you swapped some products for jewellery. The jewellery might have a significant notional monetary value, but if you cannot sell it for cash you will not be able to pay your bills in full and on time. You will be insolvent, '**asset rich, cash poor**', and will be forced out of business. I will limit myself on this one example as I deal with the issues more fully later.

c) Try to sell products which bring real benefits to your customers

As discussed in an earlier chapter, your customers buy the benefits they get from a product and not its features or perceived advantages. The maximum value of a product lies not in its technical details but primarily on the benefits it brings to the purchaser. Your company must ensure it has a committed and vibrant activity which renews and adds to your product offering. If you are not doing so, some competitor will. The people involved in creating or sourcing new or better products will not have the same personality characteristics as those involved in selling or administration.

You should therefore take great care to create a product development team that has an open-minded approach to creating new products and a budget to sustain its activities even in difficult times. The use of personality and aptitude testing will be invaluable in doing this.

Research

This is an area where accountancy can have undue influence. Firstly there is a convention to call all this activity '*Research and Development*'. However, **research** is fundamentally different to product development. Research is the process of searching for totally new and unknown materials or product applications. There is no proof that such things can exist and money spent may never be recouped. For this reason money spent on research is normally written out of the company's Balance Sheet as it is spent. This has the tax advantage that this expenditure, so expended, can be deducted from the company's tax bill and consequently becoming essentially subsidised. However this does reduce reported profits and in bad times if not fully understood such 'research' activity will be reduced or eliminated. This will damage the flow of future product innovations. Of course research if successful can result in potent new products and if truly innovative can be patented, and such patents are given a capital value far in excess of the original spending on research.

Development

Development should be seen as different. It is the creation of new or improved products by the use of KNOWN materials or processes. This is as opposed to the search for unknown factors by researchers. Most products are capable of being improved in step by step continuous improvements, and there should be highly intelligent and well-trained people to carry out this work within clearly defined expenditure budgets. It could be inferred from the above that 'products' means only physical manufactured items. However it is just as important to work in the same way with knowledge-based 'products' such as financial products and other services. They need to create an environment of continuous development.

d) Grow faster than inflation and the market sector you are in

WHY? Well, if you are not growing at least as fast as inflation you are effectively in decline, and ultimately you will become an ineffective competitor. If you are in a business sector that is growing faster than inflation you should work at maintaining your market otherwise you are in 'relative decline'. The danger in this is that your competitors may grow so much larger that they can attack you economically by offering lower prices or having greater geographic cover.

Growth is such an important and complex subject as it involves virtually every aspect of the company; consequently it is going to be dealt with more fully in a separate chapter.

e) Employ the very best people you can afford

Note especially the caveat that says *people you can afford!!!* When you are small or even just starting out you will not be able to afford the very best people. In fact, you will be the very best person you can afford for some time in the early stage of creating a new company. However, you should try to afford the best as soon as you can. It is, in my opinion, false economy to try and save money by not paying an exciting salary.

You can of course incentivise really special people to join you by offering a shareholding in the new company so that they become part owners. This can be very exciting to people who would like to have their own company but can't manage to do it themselves. Instead they can be part owners and possibly reap large benefits later if the company is very successful.

I made this a major part of my strategy at all times in my companies as they grew. I NEVER had 100% of the companies I started or acquired.

If one of my people came up with what seemed a new and exciting idea for a new product range then we formed a new company around them and gave them some share capital. We then contributed some working capital, gave them a desk and a phone, then let them get on with it, provided they followed our policies and management strategies. He was given financial support and management guidance. Of particular importance was that being within the main structure of the company if he needed help it was available at the 'next desk', so to speak. We started up many companies like this and I cannot list them all here. A lot failed, and in that case the company was wound up and the individual reabsorbed into the main company. Sometimes they wanted to leave and continue under their own resources. In which case we tried to help them do so and even in some situations maintained a minority shareholding ourselves.

A particular benefit of this process was that it was well understood and seen to happen by the whole company. This created a dynamic and exciting environment as people tried to come up with new ideas and create new companies. Sometimes where such a subsidiary became very successful we offered to swap their shares in the subsidiary for an equivalent value in the main company shares. By this method we could pour resources into a fast growing new company and remain fair to our main shareholders. It also allowed the entrepreneur to cash out if he wanted to do so.

f) Manage by objectives and build effective teams

What do I mean by *manage by objectives*? It is easier to understand if it is compared to the system used by most companies, which manage by command and threat.

Management by objectives means telling the whole company where the Board of Directors want the company to go, and the rules (mainly our seven objectives listed earlier) which have to be followed. This was the process of defining our objectives, 'Where we want to go and the rules to be followed'. We then trusted every employee to be capable of defining their own path to the main objective. They quickly found that they could not all work independently and that teams were needed for maximum capability. We used management tools to help this process. The two main ones were Personality Profiling using a commercial system supplied by Thomas Ltd and a team building process created by Professor Belbin. Once again they were available commercially. We tested people and paid for them to take training sessions at the appropriate times. I was the first to be evaluated and my results shared by the whole company. What made this very interesting was that most people, but especially those working closely with me, initially delighted in pointing out my main defects as an individual, whereas the process was designed to highlight my strengths. After all the "I told you so" calmed down then it was realised what a powerful management tool had been created. Each member of a team realised their own strengths, but most importantly the strengths of the others in the team. Yes, as my colleagues delighted in pointing out, I was very competitive and verbal. I didn't like dealing with lots of detail (unless it was vital to success). I was impatient and disinclined to listen to others. As I began to understand that these characteristics were inherent in me, I managed to ameliorate their impact on others.

On the other hand I was quick-thinking and able to express myself easily. I liked people and loved to travel. I was innovatively excited by the new. Most importantly, as one of my senior colleagues identified, I was very quick on the uptake in a new situation. I liked working in teams but wanted to be the leader. Finally, I had an outstanding visual memory. All of these characteristics came into play as my company grew on a global basis. I got others to cover my defects, and by choosing the best people, it became second nature to trust them.

g) Be good citizens and contribute to your society

This objective was intended to address the moral issues that arose in working around the world in widely differing cultures. We did not seek to impose our methodology everywhere, but rather used the local laws and behaviour patterns. One of the great insights that came to me, as the company ultimately worked in over 20 countries, was the importance of the grammatical structure of the various languages. I was and am a poor linguist, but when I became able to alter my basic English grammar to match the grammatical structure of a particular country, communication became easier. Surprisingly the USA, which speaks English, was particularly difficult to communicate with accurately. For example, I was upbraided by an American director in saying his idea was a useful one. He angrily retorted that a waste paper basket was useful, whereas his idea was GREAT. In Japanese you have to put the subject at the beginning of the sentence, and in Australia just tell it as it is.

Having taken all this on board and understood the laws and customs better, I caused less offence and avoided being misled about a business deal. I often met other businessmen on my travels who warned me about the deceitful practices by Asian companies – they were not deceitful, they were DIFFERENT.

4. WHAT TYPE OF COMPANY DO YOU WANT TO BE?

a) SOLE TRADER/SELF EMPLOYED

b) PARTNERSHIP

c) LIMITED LIABILITY PARTNERSHIP

d) FAMILY COMPANY

e) LIMITED LIABILITY COMPANY

f) COMPANY LIMITED BY GUARANTEE

g) PUBLIC COMPANY

h) COMMUNITY INTEREST COMPANY

i) CHARITY

j) THE DIFFERENCE BETWEEN DIRECTORS AND MANAGERS

This section is intended for general information rather than a detailed description including legal issues. These headings list the most important company structures and the general rules under which they operate. They will help you to consider all your options before starting. Some research using Google and especially Wikipedia will expand your understanding of these options. However, before you make a final decision, you should consult both a qualified accountant and lawyer. This advice is particularly relevant if you expect to be and remain a family company. You should pay particular attention to the differing legal responsibilities of directors, managers and shareholders. You will be able to change from one form of company to another as you progress but you should do so with proper professional advice.

a) Sole trader/Self Employed

This is the most basic form of company where an individual operates under their own name or under a separate business name. If you use a separate name you will be known as, say J Smith, trading as MAGIC HAPPENINGS. You will effectively work for yourself and be responsible for all taxes that are relevant. Of particular importance is the threshold where you have to become registered for VAT. It is very dangerous to ignore your tax liabilities. You should make every effort to understand them and pay on time. If you have difficulty, use an accountant or bookkeeper and discuss any problems with the relevant tax authority at the earliest opportunity. They will be able to advise you on how to resolve your problems.

The main advantage of being a sole trader is simplicity. You do not have to employ or manage staff. You can of course sub-contract out to others work that you cannot do yourself, even to the extent of making the product you sell or use.

The main disadvantage is the amount of time you will need to run the enterprise. This can include the time needed to sell your product. Whilst you are seeking appointments or 'doing the books', you are not carrying out your business. Time management is a vital skill.

b) Partnership

It may be that becoming a sole trader is not attractive or practical, in which case you can work with others as a partnership. Many professionals such as lawyers work in this way. Once again we urge you to get full professional advice before using this structure. There will have to be a legal document setting out the terms of the partnership, especially the financial and legal liabilities under which the Partnership will be run and managed. It is possible for one partner out of a group of partners to end up with the liabilities of the whole group.

c) Limited Liability Partnership

It is for the above difficulties that the Limited Liability Partnership structure came into being. It more clearly defines and details the liability of the Partners and, as it says, it helps limit these liabilities. It is very unlikely you will chose this structure and if you do, once again get expert help.

d) Family Company

This is not a separate legal type of company but it is a structure that suits many enterprises. A whole or part of a family may wish to work together as a family. Many famous large companies started like this and grew mightily. Others remain happily at a smaller intimate size for many generations. Real problems occur when authority is not clearly defined and written down right at the beginning. These written agreements should be fully discussed at the earliest opportunity before the event occurs and should include all the interested parties. A limited liability or even a public company can be effectively a family company, but the problems listed above will still arise. It is vital that the board and management structure are clearly agreed and listed. Nearly all family companies will have disputes and these can be fatal to the company. Proper board or management structure is essential and should be committed to paper and if necessary dated and signed. This advice may seem overly rigorous where an enterprise begins with great excitement and hope.

However problems will arise and early anticipation of them can avoid a family feud which may well occur when the company is already in difficulty.

e) *Limited Liability Company*

This is the most common type of company formed when a group of people want to work together in a joint enterprise but where responsibilities and liabilities are not to be shared equally. The company itself is owned by the SHAREHOLDERS who may own differing amounts of shares and need not work in the company, but may just supply money (capital). The company must be registered at Companies House and may be given a unique company number. The company's operation and management are detailed formally in the Memorandum and Articles of Association (Mems & Arts). If you decide to create such a company it is essential that you get full professional advice. In particular you should read in detail the proposed Memorandum and Articles of Association. If there is any dispute between members the rule written in these documents will decide who is right. There are various standard versions of these documents which must be adapted to meet your needs.

The people who intend to create such a company will do so mostly because, as it says, the investors (owners) are limiting their potential liabilities to the amount they subscribe for in shares at any time. For example, if four people wish to start a new company and are agreed on the Mems & Arts, they may decide that the company needs to have £10,000 capital to start the business. They can agree to share this sum equally between them by issuing 1000 shares valued at £10 each and each being allocated 250 shares. If at any time the enterprise fails and becomes insolvent they lose this money and no more, unless they have behaved illegally in allowing the company to fail. There is great flexibility to the number of shares that are authorised.

f) Company Limited By Guarantee

These companies are virtually identical to an ordinary limited liability company with the exception of how the shareholding is arranged. These companies are created where there is likely to be a large and changing number of shareholders, for example, in a Golf Club where each member is an equal shareholder whilst remaining as a member of the Club. Otherwise each time the membership changed, the shares would have to be sold and re-registered at the Companies House. For this reason each shareholder/member guarantees to subscribe a fixed amount of money linked to shares if the enterprise fails. This may often be as little as £1 as the member pays a substantial sum in membership fees. All the other rules of a limited liability company remain.

g) Public Company

Whilst it is true that a limited liability company

allows a great deal of flexibility in capital raising and shareholding, it nevertheless has some significant limitations. In general no one can be forced to sell their shares or buy more at a higher price. All changes must be approved by the majority of shareholders and even then there may be restrictions on what even the majority can do. These details will be in the body of the 'Memorandums and Articles' previously discussed, and is one of the reasons that all parties should read and agree them before becoming shareholders. The public company has been created to overcome these difficulties for companies that grow very large and need shareholders with deep pockets. To become a public company you need to be listed on a Stock Exchange. There are many of these and they come in a variety of size and locations with differing sets of rules. Your advisers will be able to identify the right exchange for you if you decide on this route. To be on a Stock Exchange the original shareholder must agree to sell a minimum number of shares into an open (public) market where individual holders can buy or sell them at any agreed price whenever they wish to. This arrangement enables the raising of very large sums of money for the appropriate company. As it is unlikely that you will be at this stage early on in your career, we will not spend further time covering this class of company as you will certainly need very experienced and expensive professional advisers.

h) *Community Interest Company - 'CIC'*

Due to the strong controls imposed on the charity sector, particularly that of the charity having to be run by independent unpaid trustees, there has been created the CIC structure. This is more like a normal Ltd style company but with several extra limitations. The CIC can be run by regular fully paid directors. It can buy and sell shares and pay dividends. There are however restrictions on how much can be paid in dividends and no profit can be made on the sale of shares. Otherwise it acts like a charity and should be considered if you are considering supporting some form of community work.

i) *Charity*

It may be that you want to ensure that your company carries out specific charitable activities. In this case you can set up the right structure and have your charity approved and registered by the Charity Commissioners. You will need to specify what your charitable objectives are and be prepared to ensure they are followed correctly in the operation of the charity. You will have to appoint independent trustees who cannot be paid a salary, although they can be paid approved expenses. People who work for the charity can be paid for their work. Proper accounts must be kept, audited, and reported to the Charity Commission every year.

j) Shareholders, Directors, Managers and Employees

These various descriptions have been used above in discussing company structures and it is possible that some further information will be useful.

Shareholders are the source of a company's investment in working capital. They subscribe for shares, and ownership of those shares bring considerable rights but with the risk that they can lose all of their money. They may or not work for the company depending on circumstances. If they work for the company they will become employees and may or may not be managers and directors.

Directors are appointed by the shareholders to run the company on their behalf and subject to the law must always act in the shareholders' best interests. It is not necessary for directors to hold shareholdings but it is often thought share ownership will align the directors' interests with the other shareholder. There are two main types of directors: a) *Non-Executive Directors* who serve on the Board of the company in a strategic or supervisory role but do not carry out any day to day management role, and b) *Executive Directors* who have a direct management role in the company. For example Finance Director, Sales Director, Production Director, HR Director, R&D Director, and most importantly of all the Managing Director. These executive directors have quite a balancing act. When sitting in a Board meeting they must always consider the interests of the shareholders, but at the same time are responsible for their specific management role where they report to the Managing Director, who is himself in the meeting. In order to run such a complex meeting there is a need for a Chairman to run the meeting. The Chairman, especially in smaller companies, can also be the Managing Director. This is not favoured in large companies, where these two roles are seen as separate. The Chairman's role is principally to form and run the meetings of directors, whereas the role of the Managing Director (or CEO) is to directly run the company and is held responsible for achieving the results required by the Board itself. The directors will normally meet with shareholders at the Annual General Meeting (AGM) but it can discuss issues at other times provided all shareholders are treated equally.

k) Franchising or Licensing

A completely different approach to creating a new business is offered by the two activities listed here. Franchising is a huge sector of businesses operated around the world. For example, McDonalds and Pizza Hut are franchises. In franchising the creator of the business owns the intellectual property of the new company. They create not only the product, but a whole guide book of how to prepare and sell it. They will sell the rights to a given location allowing the franchisee to set a replica business there. All the supplies will be provided by the Franchisor who also sets the prices. The franchisee runs the business according to the agreed plan and pays a royalty based upon his sales to the Franchisor. If the business does not do well then the contract can be terminated.

Many people do very well in operating a franchise and sometimes take multiple sites.

You can create your own franchising model, but remember, your idea must be powerful enough to make the profit level necessary for two levels of profit – that going to the Franchise, and that going to the Franchisor.

Licensing can often be generated from an invention, especially a patented one. In these circumstances an inventor will have created a new product and patented it, but may lack the finance or skills to make and sell it. It could be that large investments will be needed and only a larger, well-established company has the resources. It may be that the inventing person lacks the finance to defend the patent in court if a larger firm copies it. In these circumstances it may be possible to licence a larger company to make and sell it. The inventor takes royalties for every item sold and may act as a paid adviser, but he has to hand over control of the product to the third party. Obviously a strong legal contract is essential. Many such agreements are made between university research centres and large companies. Both parties concentrate on their own strengths and don't lose the focus of their core skills.

5. FINANCIAL RECORDING AND ANALYSIS

a) *Accountancy Fundamentals*

Right at the beginning of this section we would like to stress that no company can fully succeed without someone having a deep and clear understanding of accounting. Too often out of necessity and costs this work is done by a separate independent accountant who is also used as an Auditor for the preparation of tax reporting. This can lead to a culture that regards minimising (not evading!!) tax as the prime function of an accountant. The sooner you can afford your own advising accountant, the better, as there is so much more to accounting than preparing the annual accounts. As we will show later, a deep and thorough understanding of the various aspects of accounting will be immensely valuable to a business owner, especially through times of change and growth. The two main sections of accounting are straight Financial Accounting, principally aimed at Audit, and the discipline known as Management Accounting, aimed more at preparing and evaluating the financial information to be used in running the company.

The central plank of the standard financial accounting process is the Balance Sheet. It is exactly what it says, it is '*a statement at a particular specific time of the balance between what it is you have and own set against that which you owe*'.

What you own are your tangible and intangible assets + cash + money that you are owed by customers or other debtors.

What you owe will be bills from your trade creditors + any loans you have + other unpaid sums such as salaries or tax.

Later, there are given examples of a real company's Balance Sheet and another company's profit and loss account.

b) *Balance Sheet*

Virtually all companies use the same format for the presentation of their Balance Sheet, although this will become more complex with larger companies (look at the examples and identify the various sections).

FIXED ASSETS

a) Tangible assets such as property, plant and machinery, cars etc;

b) Intangible assets such as patents, software, copyrights;

c) Investments such as shareholdings in other companies or in structured financial instruments.

CURRENT ASSETS

a) Debtors (all the sums you are owed by customers);

b) Cash held in the bank or some other location such as the company's safe;

c) Stock.

CREDITORS

This includes all the money you owe to your suppliers or any other organisations which is due within a one-year time frame.

NET CURRENT ASSETS

These comprise of the current assets less the creditors. This gives you a quick look at your ability to pay your creditors if they need paying. If this becomes a negative number then you will not be able to pay due bills. You may well have to borrow against assets, but without a source of ready cash you will be in difficulty. You will be able to borrow money from your bank, who will take charge over your assets until you repay them. If you are unable to pay back the bank on the due date, you are rated as insolvent and the bank can appoint receivers to sell off the company or its assets to pay back the loan. Your company can be profitable but insolvent due to a lack of cash. A very common cause of this is to buy too much stock or sell it too slowly and be unable to pay your supplier on time.

TOTAL ASSETS LESS TOTAL LIABILITIES

This is a measure of whether the company has any value at all. If the total liabilities exceed the total assets then you are INSOLVENT and must cease trading or the directors become personally liable for any losses.

CAPITAL AND RESERVES

This is located at the bottom of a Balance Sheet and summarises the current state of the company's capital.

a) Called Up Share Capital

This is the sum of money resulting from the sale of shares in the company to its shareholders.

b) Share Premium

This identifies the sum raised by issuing extra capital products to new or existing shareholders. The price of such extra shares is not the same as the original capital shares.

c) Profit and Loss Account

This identifies the capital retained from profits not distributed as dividends.

c) Detailed Profit and Loss Accounts

The example given is for the same company used as an example for a Balance Sheet. The most useful aspect of this P/L is that it details all the likely costs you will meet in running your company. If you choose to manufacture your own products then the section labelled *costs of sales* will need expanding to cover all extra costs of manufacturing, which will be similar to the expenses listed in the example. Manufacturing costs will be dealt with in another section.

There is one heading which may need some explanation, which is:

Depreciation

This is a sum of money listed in the P/L account to facilitate the tax-free replacement of plant and machinery (including office equipment) as they age and wear out. As an example of how this works, we will identify some new computer equipment, purchased at £5000. You can expect this to last for five years before it needs replacing. Taxation rules allow you to make a charge in your P/L account of £1000 each year for its eventual replacement. After five years you will have in your balance sheet £5000 which has not been taxed to buy a replacement. This should encourage continuous investment in plant and machinery.

As there are a variety of ways this is applied, you should get expert advice from an accountant.

REAL COMPANY EXAMPLE

Balance sheet as at 31st December

	2009	2008
Fixed Assets		
Tangible assets	1,085	371
Investments	70,650	60,150
Intangible assets	71,735	60,521
Current assets		
Stocks	105,514	38,447
Debtors	0	135,129
Amount due from subsidiary company	237,450	184,537
Sundry debtors and	108	10,084

prepayments		
Cash at bank and in hand	82,309	92
	425,381	368,289

Creditors

Amounts falling due within one year	85,469	140,687
Net current assets	339,912	227,602
Total assets less current liabilities	411,647	288,123

Creditors

Amounts falling due after more than one year	(304,645)	(178,910)
Net Assets	**107,002**	**109,213**

Capital and reserves

Called up share capital	3,000	3,000
Share premium account	99,100	99,100
Profit and loss account	4,902	7,113
Shareholder funds	**107,002**	**109,213**

These details are from an actual trading company.

Profit and Loss account for the year ended 31st December

	2009	2008
Turnover	**1,056,717**	**446,819**
Cost of Sales	38,447	15,281
Opening work in progress	965,078	379,397
Closing work in progress	0	0
	1,003,525	394,678
Gross Profit	**53,192**	**52,141**
Expenses		
Staff salaries	20,859	16,088
Rent and rates	10,462	14,293
Travel expenses	8,223	54
Telephone	3,873	1,206
Bank charges and interest	3,064	1,796
Accountancy fees	2,662	2,533
Insurance	1,355	427
Training costs	1,041	250
Donations and subscriptions	1,000	0
Light and heat	885	956

Printing, post and stationary	592	241
Depreciation	542	183
Sundry expenses	301	217
Advertising	300	0
Office cleaning	213	250
Consultancy fees	39	7,694
Computer expenses	0	165
Total expenses	**55,408**	**46,353**
Profit (loss) for the previous year before taxation	**(2216)**	**5,788**
Corporation tax provision	5	1,215
Profit (loss) after tax	**(2211)**	**4573**
Retained profit (loss) brought forward	7,113	2,540
Retained profit carried forward	**4,902**	**7,113**

These numbers are from an actual operating company.

d) Management Accounting

Management accounting exists to inform and

facilitate the process of managing a company. This is as opposed to the normal accounting audit purpose of accurately identifying the financial condition of a company at a specific date and time, for example, at 0000 hours on the 31st December. There are specific professionals who only practice management accounting but do not carry out audit work. The chartered accountants who do carry out audit will also be able to deal with management accounting, but will in general not seek to go into such detail as specialist management accountants. True management accounting will concern itself more with the reasons for financial transactions and forecasting future outcomes more accurately. It is essential in running a successful, growing company to be able to guess the future of the company in as accurate a way as possible. Note we have used the words "guess the future". Nobody can forecast the future with any great accuracy, so we believe that although we use the word forecasting, we should always bear in mind that it is a guess, and the further forward a projection is taken, the less accurate it will be.

The single most important information that managing accounting provides is an accurate forecast of the cash flow in a company. As has previously been identified, lack of cash to pay creditors is a major cause of companies going out of business. There are many articles about cash flow forecasting, but the basics are simple. These are that you should create a spreadsheet which is based upon your profit and loss bookkeeping as illustrated earlier in this book. Put the P&L listings at the left hand side of the spreadsheet with columns representing months to the right of this. The spreadsheet should cover at least a

12-month period divided up into months. The P&L listings need the addition of a heading of cash alongside the one showing gross profit, and again after the one showing profit after tax.

The main figures are those derived from your sales forecast. For the first month, put in your anticipated sales, but it is vital to realise the cash element will only be in your bank when your customer pays you. This can range from cash with order/cash on delivery/cash 30 days after delivery/cash 60+ days after delivery. Thus, in your cash flow you have to put in the payment received some significant time after the invoice date.

Your cash out comprises two main elements. Those costs of making or buying your product and the costs associated with actually managing the company, normally called overheads. The costs for acquiring the product will be well in advance of your sales invoice and even further in advance of getting the cash from your customer. Your overhead costs have some fine-grain issues to take into account. The first listing should be your fixed costs. These will cover rent, insurance, light and heat, depreciation, etc. The second list will contain what are called variable costs which cover advertising, car expenses, printing, etc. You have some control over variable costs. For example, salaries can be either fixed or variable depending on the contracts you have with your employees. If you have hard times you can reduce your staffing levels fairly rapidly but you may damage your company's capabilities by doing so.

A further complication concerns charges for supplies such as electricity, gas or professional services such as audit. These may well be charged in arrears of the actual supply and you can carry out a process known as accruals. This is where you put in a notional charge into the cash flow for each month which essentially ensures you have saved enough cash to meet the bill when it arrives.

When you are starting out, this will once again be largely guesswork, but as the company survives and grows cash flow forecasts can be made very accurate. Just always remind yourself that having enough cash is vital and that you mostly have to pay out before you make any real income. There can easily be three-month gaps or more between buying the materials to invoicing and getting paid. You will need the capital or borrowing capacity to manage this gap successfully. Your overheads march relentlessly forward and keep growing. Keep them under control.

e) Forecasting

We suggest a particular approach to forecasting that has proven effective over a long period of time. It accepts that errors increase with time and puts in techniques to accommodate them. Despite banks and other organisations demanding sales and profit forecasts from start-up or new-ish companies, the fact is they will only ever be best guesses. Realistic forecasting can only be done with some three or more years of factual accounts. Why three? If you project the next year after two years by drawing a line through the existing outcomes you will probably draw a straight line. It is unlikely that a new (or any) company will grow on a straight-line basis. The third year gives an indication as to whether a company is accelerating or slowing down. Further years will give clearer and clearer indications.

We suggest that the best forecasting method is to work on a combined monthly and annual basis. We also believe that graphical representations of the data will help inform the human judgement that is involved. Supposing then that we have three years' accurate monthly data supplied by the management accountants. These will contain in the monthly information: a) the sales volume, b) the overhead costs, c) the gross and net profit, d) the cash available to run the business, e) the order input. These are the prime measurements that will need supervision to run the company successfully.

Each of these should be used to create separate graphical representations of each measurement. Monthly graphs can vary wildly, especially in the early life of a company and there are various methods to smooth out these variations. Two most commonly used are a three-month (quarterly) moving average and an annual moving average. In each case the first number that is plotted is at the end of the specified period. For example, with the quarterly graph the first three months of data are added together and divided by three, giving an average monthly figure which is plotted for the third month of the period. At the end of the next month the same process is carried out, but this time the number is plotted monthly. In this way individual variations will be reduced, allowing any continuing trends to be identified. The same process can then be used for a moving annual total. Starting with the last year's figures you can deduct the last month's performance in the old year and add the first month's performance in the new year, and once again do that monthly. This should help smooth out most short term and seasonal effects.

Having created these graphs it should be possible to draw a trend line on a 'best fit' basis. If working with a computer programme these facilities may well be built in. Once having identified the best fit it will probably be some form of curve (hopefully upwards). It may be accelerating or decelerating and this will be obvious to a human eye. Having done so, you can forecast by projecting this graph forward at the same rate into the future. A one-year prediction will be reasonably accurate, with increasing uncertainty against time. All such forecasts should be reviewed on a monthly basis and any major new trends brought into the calculations.

To allow uncertainty to be considered, each of the annual projections should be accompanied by a graph showing a better performance, and one showing a worse outcome. This gives a likely spread to consider what implications there will be for each outcome. Fast growth may need more cash and people, whereas a slower growth can generate cash but result in lower profits and the need to reduce investments in plant machinery and people.

These are only some suggestions to help basic forecasting but remember, they are still guesses – be mentally prepared to deal with changing outcomes.

6. HOW WILL YOU KNOW WHEN YOU ARE SUCCEEDING?

The statements below are true and you are ready for the next challenge.

a) You are making more money than you spend;

b) You earn more than others will pay you;

c) When you have reached your main personal objective (listed in 1);

d) *When you can say 'yes' to all the above and are HAPPY and CONTENTED.*

7. DO YOU WISH TO CONTINUE OR EXIT AND DO SOMETHING ELSE?

Exiting from a company you have created and built can be quite complex, depending on what type of company it has become. This is especially true if you have independent shareholders or family members who disagree with you.

a) **SELL your company or your stake to another company or individual (children?)**

If this is a complete break you will have to be certain that two things at least are true. (1) You have something else to do that will satisfy you mentally. (2) You make enough money out of the deal for a secure future, especially if inflation re-occurs.

b) **MERGE with another company and stay on employed by the new entity.**

A merger is a very complex business and you must take advice both from accountants and lawyers. Both the financial terms and your personal future must be clearly and fully established and confirmed in legal form.

c) **SELL all the assets of the company and close it down?**

Some acquirers prefer this method as it avoids any undisclosed liabilities arising after the deal is finalised. Your requirement is that there is no such undisclosed liability because as a director you can become liable even if you have sold the assets.

d) **FLOAT the company on a stock exchange.**

This can make you very rich but you will have quite demanding new shareholders and very onerous reporting requirements. There are several types of stock exchanges both in the UK and abroad, so detailed research will be needed. If successful it can be the most exciting and rewarding experience. If it fails it will happen publicly and you as a director will be held liable.

ADDENDUM

This section lists all the companies I worked for and those that I created. I hope that by listing these in some detail with my various experiences it will help you have confidence in my advice. My working life encompassed a variety of experiences both practical and academic. I not only started many companies I worked for a range of very different companies in a variety of roles both junior and senior. Good luck in your ventures.

1. Cliff – The Business Creator

Starting February 1972

- PERDIX COMPONENTS Ltd – Importing Trading company, £3,000 capital

  Specialised in displays, electronic components,

power supplies, analogue computing modules.

By 1974 added:

- TAYLOR MILLER Ltd – Holding company, £10,000 capital;

- RBS COMPONENTS Ltd – Manufacturer of High-Tech Capacitors;

- NORE MICROWAVE Ltd – Manufacturer of Advanced Microwave Components;

- VIDEOTONE Ltd – Importing and Design company, audio products.

Trading with, Japan, Taiwan, USA, France, Hungary, India.

By 1984 added:

- MARCH MICROWAVE – Microwave Manufacturing and Trading company;

- KENTEC – Specialised Electronic Trading Company;

- ART COMMUNIQUE – Artwork and Publishing company. Joint venture;

- VT COMPUTERS Ltd – Computer Manufacturing and Trading company.

By 1986 Floated on main Stock Exchange, market value £10 million

ALL the above companies, plus added:

- DENSITRON JAPAN Ltd – Export Trading company;

- DENSITRON AMERICA Ltd – Importing Sales company;

- DENSITRON EUROPE Ltd.

By 2000 added:

- DENSITRON TAIWAN Ltd – Exporting Trading company;

- HIGHTEC TAIWAN Ltd – Displays Manufacturing;

- DENSITRON FRANCE Ltd – Sales company;

- SKYLAB Ltd, Italy – Sales company;

- ACTRON Ltd, Germany – Sales company;

- DENSITRON Australia – Sales company;

- FERROGRAPH Ltd – Large Outdoor Displays Manufacturer;

- FORWARD ELECTRONICS, Taiwan – Joint venture, Manufacturing Volume Displays in China;

- AGENTS in Norway, Denmark, Finland, Sweden, Belgium, South Africa, Greece, Spain;

- TRADING PARTNERS in Israel, Russia, Brazil, India.

By 2002 – Retired

Started:

- DIGITAL CONNECTIONS EUROPE Ltd;

- DIGITAL DISPLAYS EUROPE Ltd;

- DIGITAL DISPLAYS FRANCE Ltd;

- MRCE Ltd;

- CYTECH Ltd.

- Acted as BUSINESS ADVISER to around 30 companies;

- Was CHAIRMAN of GOVERNERS to two secondary schools, duration over 25 years;

- Was REGIONAL CHAIRMAN of CBI;

- Was on the BOARD of EEF;

- Currently the CHAIRMAN of KENT SEARCH AND RESCUE.

2. Cliff's Life – Working for Others 1953-1972

My working life began in the RAF, doing two years of National Service.

This period laid the real foundations and direction of my future career in electronic engineering. I had attended Addey & Stanhope Grammar School in Deptford from 1945 to 1953 with only moderate success. I obtained a School Certificate in some five subjects and 'A' levels in physics and chemistry. Grammar schools were primarily aimed at academic capability, with just a nod towards skills through woodwork. There was no understanding of applied sciences such as engineering.

Joining the RAF changed all that. Right at the

beginning they carried out two weeks of what they called Trade Tests but which in fact were aptitude tests. These spotted me in clear ability in engineering and public speaking. They didn't explain all this at the time, it is only afterwards I realised what the process had been. After basic training (square bashing), lasting two months, I was posted to RAF Locking to train as a Ground Wireless Fitter (command). At the time I was very worried as I didn't have any idea what this meant. In reality it was a university level crash course in communications engineering, both theoretical and practical. It took eight months of 44-hour weeks of intensive learning. For the first time in my studying I clearly understood with rising excitement what was being taught. My physics 'A' level came in very handy.

We were tested every month and you had to pass with 80% marks or were held back for the next month's class. If you failed again you were out. A final exam allowed you to go into real work at an RAF operational station. I was posted to a new training school to teach the course I had just completed. I had the rank of Junior Technician which ultimately rose to Acting Corporal paid. I refused Acting Corporal unpaid on the advice of my father who had served in the Royal Navy.

Before I taught, however, I was sent on a three-week course on how to teach. As a teacher I had a new class every month and they were tested as I had been every month. Not only did I have to get at least 80% through the course, I had to predict the scores of every student with an accuracy of 80% or I was sent for retraining.

At this point I understood the whole process. It

was set up to succeed and failure was not tolerated. We were selected and tested at every stage, starting with educational capability followed by aptitude tests and rigorous professional standards. Ultimately I used similar techniques in setting up my own company, to which I added various skills learnt in working for other companies. The principles were: (1) a large pool to select from, (2) well educated in the fundamentals, (3) detailed aptitude analysis (4) concentrated from well-focused training, (5) high standards and (6), clear objectives.

I never again worked for a company that applied ALL these steps, although Hewlett Packard came close. Mostly companies tried to recruit the ideal person from another company who had done the training.

MULLARDS

When I left the RAF I joined Mullards (part of Philips) as a technical assistant in one of their Applications Laboratories. They went for my 'A' levels with only a limited interest in my RAF experience. Mullards manufactured thermionic valves and the lab's job was to design advanced circuitry to be given free to manufacturers of television and audio products. I didn't mind the low starting level as the work was very interesting, being involved in the then new technology of Hi-Fi. At first this was only mono but then eventually stereo came in and sound engineering became cutting-edge with television in the consumer electronics industry. Mullards were a highly successful company and a pleasure to work for. They were hierarchical and paternalistic. I was allowed to have a day off per week without loss of wages to do further study and gain extra qualifications. Advancement in Mullards was very firmly based upon educational standards, with high level graduates the most prized. Much of the work was analytical and not creative. I happened to be more interested in new developments. This ultimately led to slow promotion and lower pay. As a result I left to join the Westinghouse Brake and Signal Company at a much higher salary.

My LESSONS from Mullards were that:

1. Developing markets had to be fed with modern products but at low risk;

2. A fixed employee structure could overlook creativity;

3. Paternalism did not replace people management.

WESTINGHOUSE

I actually joined a subsidiary of the main Westinghouse company with the outstanding name of W.R. Sykes Interlocking Signal Company Ltd, who were the original inventors of the mechanical '*Lock and Block*' mechanical railway signalling system. They had been taken over by Westinghouse and expected to develop new businesses. I was their first modern recruit and got the job primarily because of my experience at Mullards in working with then revolutionary transistors.

Both Westinghouse Brake and Signal and W.R. Sykes were poorly run companies with no real business focus. They had mostly focussed on railway signalling on a cost plus method of pricing for contracts. They desperately desired a new and competitive range of products but there was no proper management structure that I could understand.

In retrospect I learnt a great deal from my work there but it was principally 'what NOT to do'. It was only much later working at Hewlett Packard that I identified the failings. At the time I was very happy in my work.

The main LESSONS were that:

1.   You had to understand your market;

2.   You had to develop new competitive products on a continuous basis;

3.   You had to have an aggressive and well-focussed sales force;

4.   You needed a well thought-out employee strategy;

5.   You need to make money, 'profits', if you are to exist and compete.

LEMCO

Joining LEMCO was both a tremendously valuable lesson and a bad mistake. It was a family firm focussed on low-cost capacitors for the consumer electronics industry. It was very efficient and sold mostly on price. The founding father who had started the business died suddenly and there was no family member ready to take over. As a result the company was being run by the existing Board of Directors who, as far as I could tell, were primarily interested in their own rewards rather than the health of the company. They had decided to get into more advanced products rather than having to compete in the cut-throat consumer market. They had advertised for a Technical Marketing Manager to identify and develop new product ranges. I wanted to leave Westinghouse due to salary uncertainty. The Lemco post seemed and was a step towards moving to a sales career. I successfully identified new products and markets for the modern industrial electronics companies. Unfortunately they demanded much higher production standards and the Board of Directors chose to cut corners. So much so that they delivered a sequence of poorly made batches to a large electronic manufacturer. They demanded we took them back and we were refusing. The directors ordered me to go some 60 miles by car to persuade the customer to accept our product. I protested that there was no way to make the delivered batches suitable for the customer and that we should have to take them back. Nothing I said persuaded them, they were stuck in the past. I went to the customer, who demonstrated the product deficiencies that made them unusable. I agreed with them and loaded them into my car to take them back. I went directly home and looked for job adverts in selling. I knew I had no future at Lemco.

Coincidentally Hewlett Packard, who were at that time the world's top electronic measuring instrument manufacturer, were advertising for a sales engineer in my area. I applied for it and got it, albeit at a lower salary than at Lemco. In retrospect I had learnt some valuable lessons at Lemco; these were: (1) a family company without the family involved can be usurped by inadequate managers, (2) you can't mix high quality and cheap products, (3) you must never feel you can con your customers and (4) you must have and listen to properly qualified staff!

HEWLETT PACKARD

It is very important to realise that this HP was not what it eventually became (a global computer company). They did introduce the first HP computers in my time with them but they were aimed at supporting the instrument market. HP was by far the best company I ever worked for and I modelled my own company very much on their principles. They consciously sought out and attracted the best talent available. They had a printed set of six objectives by which they ran the firm. They paid well but expected your total attention to their success. Both Hewlett and Dave Packard visited each of their locations regularly and talked to whoever they met. They would ask questions and expect accurate truthful replies; they would answer your questions in return. They trained staff constantly and rewarded achievement. They aimed to put their factories where people wanted to work rather than where was cheapest. They fostered internal and external competition. In management terms for us salesmen, we were set challenging targets on a daily, weekly, monthly and annual basis. You were expected to exceed all of them.

Ultimately what caused me to leave was that although there was all this excitement, they tended to own you. If it was Saturday and they wanted you in Geneva on Sunday, you went. Your wife got a box of chocolates on the Monday. Eventually it became clear that I might be asked to go to the USA with no guarantee that I could return to the London area. At that precise time I was head-hunted by a medium-sized family company who were looking for a Marketing Director. I was very flattered at the invitation and attended interviews by the Board and the head-hunters. I would initially be paid less than at HP but I would be given a 10% stake in the company through a shareholding and would be made a director after a one-year probationary period. I accepted.

The LESSONS I learnt from HP were many but the main ones were:

1.   Clear objectives,

2.   Training,

3.   Involvement by the owners,

4.   High quality managers,

5.   The importance of organised competitive sales forces,

6.   Constant measurement of performance,

7.   Good rewards.

KGM

This was another mistake that I have learnt a great deal from. KGM were a small manufacturer of electronic displays and CCTV equipment. This was back in the late sixties and so we were very advanced for the time. They had **iii** as an investor and once again they needed to update their product range and sales procedures. They had shown me their production graphs which showed considerable growth. Unfortunately they did not reveal their considerable decline in new orders. A fact I only realised many months later after I had, by hand, gone through the files and added up the past two years' monthly order input. The shock was very real and I went straight to the MD, who said that was the reason they had hired me, but they had been reluctant to tell me in case I didn't take the job. By now I had a wife and child, plus a mortgage to support, I couldn't back out. By what were great strokes of luck and no little intelligent hard work I reversed the situation within about 18 months. I went to the Board and requested the promised directorship and shareholding. Their response was that because of my successful actions the shares were now too valuable to give me the promised 10% stake. In fact I would get nothing. I appeared to get the directorship but actually it was phony. I was in a quandary. I felt that if I changed jobs too much and returned to engineering as such would condemn me to a work life of mediocrity and boredom. At that point I was directly offered a job near home at a higher salary. It seemed heaven sent but in fact, was the final bad decision that sent me on the right path at last, and I started my own company.

What had I LEARNT from KGM?

1. The biggest lesson was to ensure that any important promises were confirmed in writing;

2. I learnt about international trade and importing;

3. I made an enduring link to Japan that underpinned all the following successes;

4. I learnt how to exploit the technical press;

5. I learned a little about bookkeeping and accounts;

6. I learned about branding.

GUEST INTERNATIONAL

The final mistake, but the one that finally drove me into depression and ultimately to come out of it by starting my own company. I learned little from Guest other than to always treat people with respect.

CONTACT INFORMATION

cliff@dcel.co.uk
www.dcel.co.uk
153 Main Road
Biggin Hill
Kent
TN16 3JP